AGAMEMNON'S POPPIES

AGAMEMNON'S POPPIES

ADRIENNE EBERHARD

Black Pepper
Melbourne, Australia

First published by *Black Pepper*
403 St George's Road, North Fitzroy, Victoria 3068

National Library of Australia
Cataloguing-in-Publication data:

      Eberhard, Adrienne
      Agamemnon's poppies
      ISBN 1 876044 40 3

      I.   Title

A821.4

Cover design: Gail Hannah

This project has been assisted by the Commonwealth Government through the Australia Council, its art funding and advisory body.

Acknowledgements

Grateful acknowledgement is made to the editors of the following publications in which many of these poems first appeared, some in slightly different forms:

The Australian: 'Mountains'
Belly: 'Miracle'
The Canberran: 'Dover Scallops'
The Canberra Times: 'Eating the Firmament'
Famous Reporter: 'Books for Dreaming'
Island: 'West Coast,' 'At Land's End,' 'Delusions,' 'Awakening,' 'The Cleopatra Poems,' 'Roots,' 'Lines from the Black Sea'
Poetrix: 'Voyages of Discovery,' 'Courting Paradise Rifle Bird,' 'In the Bath'
Siglo: 'Meditative Sonnets'
Southern Review: 'Bathwater, Rainwater'
Southerly: 'Coracles,' 'Coastlines,' 'Stone Boat'
Voices: 'Absence'

'Hurt' has been broadcast by the ABC on PoeticA, Radio National. 'Amphibian,' 'Absence,' 'Mycenae' and 'Wedding Dress' are included in the anthology, *Moorilla Mosaic* (eds. Lyn Reeves and Robyn Mathison, 2001). 'Jack Carington Smith' was published in the 2000 Tasmanian Poetry Festival Program.

I'd like to thank Geoff Page and Andrew Sant for their encouragement and advice; Andrew and Judith Beveridge for their help in finalising the manuscript; Noelene and Robert van Schie for nurturing a love of words and books, as well as a deep respect for Tasmanian places; and special thanks to Rolan for his abiding love and support.

Adrienne Eberhard was born in Dover, Tasmania, in 1964. She holds an MA in English on twentieth century travel writing, and has travelled herself in Europe, Asia and the Pacific. She has taught primary school in Papua New Guinea, as well as English and creative writing in Canberra and Tasmania. She lives on the D'Entrecasteaux Channel, south of Hobart, with her husband, two young sons and dog, Mungo.

for Rolan, with love

CONTENTS

I

II

III

IV

I

Roots

This tree is ancient
its trunk as grey as stones or the pitch lining hulls of
    ships
deep underneath us it must run its anchors in the earth
locking against the vast weight of soil
rock catching the heavy list and lean of it, holding it still

high in the canopy it's all at sea
sailing the threading blue, leaning in the light
mimicking the curved globe of the sky

the leaves rustle like canvas
spin and trip in the wind

only the figure-head is absent
- nameless, silent -
how can a woman feed on air and salt alone?

I want to tap the earth
send out shoots and tips and long runners
scenting through the grass and soil
to where water runs darkly, silently

and feeds me
with the sweet, cold
taste of home.

Voyages of Discovery

I

High on the sides of that dark hill
we lay nestled under sleeping bags,
bare boards fanning out all around us
like a ship's hull,
the rafters and tin roof
cracking and straining as if at sea.
The wind threw its weight against the walls,
blew hurricane breath under the door
and we lay,
coiled and tense at first,
then easy with the skin of the other.
As the sky swelled
and trees drowned in the gathering clouds,
snow piled up at the door.
I remember his lips were cool as pools
of dark water,
his fingers fed my breasts
and our bodies slipped like fishes
in the bright stream of our makeshift bed.

II

If you continue around the headland
you come to Tasman's Monument -

once those sails, huge as albatross wings,
floated the distance, driven blue
with salt and the thin, dreaming sky -

here on this beach, with his hair
streaming across my body,
loose, sifting grains at my back,
and the slow, spinning of the world,
hakea, boulder, pebble, sand,
dissolved to water, wave, horizon, sky
and I, lying still,
watching his dark eye absorb mine,
his mouth urgent as the sun's pull:

the clouds above us were wings,
were sails, and we were new arrivals,
our skins' imprint faint
as the scent of eucalypt
on the waves.

Amphibian

Frogs are singing in our neighbours' yard
as you take me in your gentle arms,
I hear their voices lifting in their throats;
a private choir of haunting, polished psalms.

They usher in dark stars and the threaded sky,
conjuring still and scented summer nights -
we open wide our window to the air,
our bodies turn golden in the waning light.

I have watched you swim with finned feet,
as poised and certain as a fish,
it seemed you'd found your natural element,
as though for water, was all you ever wished.

You hung suspended, washed by waves,
as though the world above could never be
precious or liquid, languid or potent;
you loved the very motion of the sea.

And when we lie naked in this room,
I listen to their song and feel your heart
with its rhythmic beat, its rapid pace;
I feel your smooth body slip and dart.

You are gone, back to the fluid depths,
your skin is cool, your fingers pale and webbed,
you sweep me with you in your watery dance,
outside, the melodic notes rise, then ebb.

The Cleopatra Poems
If it be love indeed, tell me how much
(Antony and Cleopatra, I, i)

sex

I'd be a boy for you
white hips plunging against yours
my wet sap filling your veins

I'd feed you lolling grapes
let you taste the sweetness of mine
lower their dangling cluster to your mouth

My tongue would shower trails of comet dust
your eyes would be the blue shoot of stars
together we would hurtle into the hot breath of space

pearls

see this small pearl
    balancing
       glistening
rolling to roundness on a grass spear

let me swallow it
feel the cool slip of it arcing in my throat

      breaking the drought

river games

I'll offer you this breast
take its pebble-paleness
and place it against your lips
feel its frailty
its river-worn whiteness
give it the cool water of your mouth
let it sink to the centre
let it drown in the waving fronds of your throat

siren

at the heart of you there's pale ambergris
this sticky substance
pooling on my skin

fashion it into the glint of jewels
to wink at my throat
to bead my hips

wrap it round me like ropes of sea-wrack
let it glow pale and golden
against the amber of my skin

gifts

I'd give you Egypt
this brown and green land
stretching   undulating

can't you see?
the Nile is in flood
it is bursting   raining   churning

oh how my body burns
this hot pulse
this fevered skin
the land is drying up
sweltering under icy sun

let me give you Egypt
it lies here wrapped in cool sheets

come
     enter Egypt

take what is yours

Absence

for Rolan in Nepal

Small green peas clatter like beads,
scattering like water drops on my plate:
they run in every direction, reckless
and unheeding, just like the jostling
thoughts in my head, of you.
The peas are round as river boulders:
stones shaped by ice and meltwater,
smoothed to the sheen of marbles,
looming large like granite lumps
spilt by glacier, dumped by avalanche.
Your dark figure weaves its way
through a shattered boulder field,
fingers glancing off smooth rock,
feet grinding against grain and pebble
as loose and slippery as rolling peas.
The peas on my plate are polished
like glass, green-bottled, cut with water;
they are the rounds you reach for
in the rushing stream, collect carefully
in your bare palm, store in your pocket.
Do you think of home as you rough
them in your grasp, clasp their coldness
against your skin, remembering
window sills of gathered shells,
broken china, pieces of stone?

The peas rub silken against my tongue,
cold and hard as a sucked pebble, but
explode with sweetness, sharding like rock;
the pale greenness of them lingers
like the memories tumbled in your pocket.

Heaven: An Elephant Love Song

Come with me my love
come with me to the Vale of the Elephants

wear your dusty hide my way
follow the wail of your trunk
wallow your belly in the mud of my passing

swat the sky with your ebony tail
roll wide your black rosary eyes
flap your ears in the sailing wind

Elephant heaven in a peanut-coloured valley
opalescent rocks that rise like sighs
in the lifting heat of an African sky

bare your belly skin to the languid air
trumpet your beauty heavenward
stamp your delight in the hot earth

sway your hips eastward, seaward
shimmy your toes in pools of blue
lift your lashes to the lapis lazuli sea

but follow me, come with me
to the Vale of the Elephants.

Courting Paradise Rifle Bird

Slow rainwaiting,
steady blood-beat of water,
black, warm, wet:
time-unfurl of feathers,
prance, swirl,
head-high,
my fan dance.
Feather-cloak of blackness,
feet-clack, castanet-clack
and crack of wings,
cymbal clashings; black.
Dark villain!
Sweep, bend and puff,
chest-flourish,
fan panning wide,
swallow deep: blue-ruff,
ring beads of light, rising,
swelling to shine, wink
at throat, chest stones,
all mine!
Blue sequins thrum,
swelling, humming,
blue flash, kingfisher-flash,
dart, plunge, float,
fall of feather,
my wings, swift circle

of blackness, darkness
framing my throat.
Dandy-black, dark angel,
whoo-ah-whi, whoo-ah-whi!
Quick as a whip,
hot, darting,
head-turning,
sharp as shot.
Crack! Crack!
Oh curve of beak,
loved one,
step side, step here,
come circle - see!
Step, step close,
catch my blue flash,
the dark slide of me.

Flight

Your face is like a statue's,
lidded, cool, gazing serenely
at the sunlight and leaves
like the clear-eyed chariot driver
in the Delphi Museum, who's chased
speed and light for the past 2000 years.

All I can see is your face on the pillow,
sharp chisel of chin,
smooth plane of cheek,
catching the light and pale sun;
a ribbon of it curls in the window
like the whip he once held.

Your bodies share the same flex
and urge and abandon,
limbs made for sudden speed;
it waits under the skin,
reined in, held back
for the last leaping burst.

I remember his eyes best,
their whiteness and shine -
as if holding secrets Icarus sought -
my eyes came back to him time after time,
seeking him amongst the statues of stone

as if he were made of flesh.

I was sure when the rooms emptied
and darkness drummed at the window,
sun would fire in his veins
and he'd wake to choked shouts, cracking whips;
his limbs would unravel and stretch
in a pulse of speed.

I see your body stir,
skin bared, muscles shifting,
watch your eyes whiten in the light,
I move closer, nestling against
breathing skin that is not bronze,
wanting this warm, human flight.

Jack Carington Smith: Simpson's Bay
for Corinne Robinson

Pale watery brush strokes,
paper curling at the edges,
and this bay a halved apricot
with gleaming flesh bared,
small pearls of moisture glisten
like beads or grains of sand.
Here there are ripples,
skin-coloured ridges,
the sea caught in troughs
then escaping in long, liquid strokes
away from the eye.
And there, distant, tall,
the Cape rises,
smooth brushes of orange and brown,
but always the eye is drawn back
to oyster-grey water,
the luminous bay;
just like the slow tugging of the tide,
the pull of the moon.

———————

White cottage, pale fields,
lucent bay like a crescent moon
or the curve of a breast.

You, bare and clean
as the sand itself,
shifting on the stool.
The paint drying,
the charcoal lines
cusping paper and skin:
your outline, the shades and shadows
of your body falling dark,
like wet footprints at low tide.

The Garden

I

In this garden there is another -
one with fretted light
and haloes of sound,
where the leaves lean to rustle and swing,
greenness leaps
and the shadows are bones of song.
This is my walled garden
surrounding a palace:
hear the soft thud of 'paradesh'
like small apples hitting the grass.

II *Ophelia*

sweet breath
sweet rue
this could be Ophelia's song
the drowning lilt of notes
turning and falling
swallowing water and water
mouthfuls
of clear, sweet utterances

oh my dearest
when you are betrayed
go to the garden
find the gathering richness
the blooming warmth
of petal, seed, husk
leaf, branch, trunk

there is such calm and emptiness
in the brushed greenness of the long grasses

III *Vita Sackville-West*

I wanted white
whiteness that is a thrust like bone
or else a shimmering haze
an insect-dance

white   white
layers of it
filling the empty spaces
all the angels massing
burning haloes
a blazing light
to match the fast fall of the moon

here the pale creep of violets
here the white blush of virgin roses
all my darlings
blooming pale and night-cool
to match the syllables of Sissinghurst.

IV *Nebuchadnezzar's Persian wife*

my mountain princess he calls me
his *little one far from home*
and I, crying for the dark trees
the winter snows
the water running clear and sharp as a knife

he brings me gifts
but nothing compares
to the cool fan of evening air
the green crooks and hollows
the lustrous shadows of these plants
as they grow
taking flight over Babylon

every day the slaves bring water
it rises slowly above the city
the pale snake of the Euphrates
feeding my garden

my veins grow strong as roots
my skin feints the brush of dew
my hair hangs soft like fern fronds
my blood stills to greenness

such radiance, such aureoles of light
here, close to Persia
close to Paradise

II

Dover Scallops

At the docks
boats ply their wares
salt water dark as velvet
scent of the sea rising with every slow wave
that pungency lifting -
and nestling in the trays, resting on ice
are rows of creamy scallops
edges overlapping, fatly, richly
orange hearts like sickled suns.
They pour off the scoop into the waiting bag
sliding like a receding tide
over pale sand
their softness bunches and pouches
in a heavy mound
that hanging weight like grapes
or tender breasts.
And in them is the sea
cold ocean
currents and tides and eddies
the pouring constancy of water
feeding them, fattening them.
Taste Dover salt
green water
dark kelp
swift shadow of albatross
Antarctic cold
and the sweet southerly whip of wind.

Meditative Sonnets on Voices, Bones

I

How many times in a paddock
have you found a finger of bone,
stumbled across its pale spareness
amongst sharp grasses or small stones.
Picked and worn smooth by beak and rain,
its hard curves softened and sunlit,
bleached and bared in the thin, loose soil;
the greyish-white cleanness of it.
Or digging deep in the garden,
fingers fumbling in the rich earth,
the soil raked over and turned,
to find moon-like shards in the turf.
Pale nubs like mushrooms, but colder:
harder, whiter, so much older.

II

There are whale skulls in your cupboard,
their porous, pumice-like greyness pared,
their long bones white and brittle - you
found them singing in the cold air
on a long, white sickle of beach,
the siren wind poured through sockets,
slid through the small, crooked spaces -
next to them cartwheels and pockets
of spine spoke the silence of the shelf;
off the south-east coast you'd seen whales,
heard their dark passage, the slide of skin
like the flap of wind in a sail.
Immersed in limpid air and blue,
you must have heard the voices too.

III

In the dark, drowning west coast lakes
there are marble museums of trees
turned still and stone-like, grim and grey
in a watery, funeral frieze.
They are silent, white skeletons
making a last, defiant stand
against mortality, waving
their bones like coral or dead men's hands.
If you swim on the lake surface
and peer through the dark tannin glow,
ghostly limbs lie at angles, trunks
gleam and your moon-white body slows:
feels tugged and pulled deep down, *deep down*,
to their leached, quiet grave, to drown.

IV

In the undergrowth there are voices,
soft, softer than the rustle of silk
or the barefoot tread of shadows,
softer even than the drowning lilt
of words in deep water. The voices
are small mouthfuls of sky, they're spare
and blue as light itself, sipping
and falling like a thread of air.
The fragile wind is caught in them,
is rolled in the blueness to breath,
tuned to the rustle of paperbark,
to the thrusting prickle of heath.
These voices flourish in shade or sun,
they're flesh and sinew; solid as bone.

Bathwater, Rainwater

Lying here in deep water
I feel myself at the bottom of the ocean,
lashed by winter storms,
rolling over and over like an abandoned shell
cast here and there by swell and current.
Outside the wind roars in the trees
and rain tumbles down endlessly,
driving at the leaves, the earth,
striking at the soil, pounding pebbles,
stones, boulders and cliffs;
washing the world away.
The whole world is a river,
sloshing and bucketing,
tea-stained, dark and turbulent.
It drags my dissolving body
down the drain of the bath,
through the plughole in smaller and smaller pieces,
out into the pipes and channels,
the storm water drains, gathering force
and freedom along with all the leaves
and small stones that tumble with me.
We collect the mud and dirt,
the silt, the gravel, all the debris
and cast-offs, out, out into the blackness,
the darkness, the wet soak and roll
of water. Unleashed, abandoned;

gaining strength,
joining forces,
until gutter meets creek, meets stream,
meets river.
All this mad jostling, this sloshing
and lively banter, we careen and join,
splashing and splitting; fluidity and motion.
We spread and spread, puddling at the edges,
running, creeping over the land.
Out, out to the horizon
until the river's in the sky -
water staining and spreading,
threading to whiteness,
to thinness and greyness, and then,
great swoop and plummet
and raining, raining down
on the leaves,
the roofs,
the windows,
the soil,
under sills,
under doors,
drop by drop
warmly,
wetly,
filling the metal sinks,
the green baths.

At Land's End

The land ends like a bruised shadow -
Icarus fallen, his body tumbled
in green depths, here the pelvis,
here the groaning shoulders,
toes reaching to the depths of the spinning sea.
At midday this flesh is molten gold
just as when he arched to touch the sun,
feathered, winged, falling.

His bones are laid bare
by tide and the sea's locking jaws.
Tendrils of hair turned to kelp,
secret hollows the haunt of fishes.
Out there his spirit washes,
whispers words, waltzes in the green light
and this land is caught gleaming
in a net, drowning.

Light beats from slow clouds,
darting like a host of fish, swamping
the day in silver insistence, in silence.
Once his surprised mouth rent the air
as he passed the tilled fields, the fishermen,
left them behind for the edge of the world.
Here at land's end in the green light,
the silver shallows, is Icarus, drowning.

West Coast: Wreck Bay to Port Davey

Pale bays lie like silver-faced spoons,
handles dissolved in the wash of spume
and sea. Their surfaces bear the marks of runes,
etched by twig, weed and broken shell,

which are sea-tossed, wind-driven, to land
in careless patterns, meandering paths,
piled high and precarious on the sand:
reminders of a world away where waste

is more than dead leaves, seaweed clumps
cast like vines, pebbles smooth as bone
and sharp, or slumped dunes, their bumps
and hollows making shadows in early afternoon.

The round nest of one bay harbours a graveyard
of rope and plastic - the scattered shellfish,
hand-picked bone of an ancient feast, lie charred
and buried by this unknowing tide.

Yet the coast escapes to reveal smoothed shells
scraped clean - faint lavender designs
eroded by wind, grain, wave, rain, swell -
placed, just so, by a careless and extended hand.

Some beaches stretch with naked stones
uniformly round and polished as ostrich eggs.
Even these reveal design. A lengthy loan
from nature for makeshift shelter.

Low oval walls (placed how long ago?),
the middle scooped, hollowed and lined;
they stand sentinels of a past, so
little understood, when these shores

knew only the rough scent of woodsmoke, fat,
wet peat, the flowering of native grasses,
the quiet cadence of language as people sat
to eat by a fire and build myths about the stars.

Ariel's Realm

dreaming of escape
an island like Prospero's
where voices leap and echo
enchantment is the colour of the sky
the scent of freesias
blue as hyacinths
take me there
by sail or wing
lift me up
let my body disperse
like motes of air
notes of song
let me shift to particles
absorb the roughness of bark
to slip inside the pine like Ariel
let me feel the green of needles
the skin like petals
or taste sand grains between my teeth
let the sea's azure
wash me to pieces
let me turn to the fluidity of water
to run and drop
sparkling like a star's tail end
let the scent of spring grass
leap at me
let me be a leaf

frail and aching
all of me trembling
with a wild awakening
to the blood-rush of myself

Eating the Firmament

this blueness is sweet as breath
it hugs the hills
the rocks
softening their hard edges
filling up the pores and crevices
with spores of lapis lazuli

imagine them nestled
against granite crystals
blue enough to put under your tongue
and suck
bluer than the patches of alpine daisies
bluer than eyes   than the sea
blue enough to fill your skin with wings

to send you wind-blown and buoyant
whisper-thin and threading
sailing up from the tor
from the hard fastness of stone
from the angled fixity of rock

into the open-mouthed sky

Crows:

absolute blackness
like soot or ink
circling high ground
capes flapping madly
magicians with ragged wings

sounds that are slightly flat
like small children crying
                    . caught

hugging high exposed places
grassy alpine fell-land
where rocks are ancient
as though in frost/rain/sun
they've absorbed history

crows feed on this
as well as plump moths
snatched in sharp beaks
feathers sleek with knowledge

hopping amongst daisies
shadows flash against stone
their black fleetness
a singing of thin air

Salmon Farm

Threads of light sweep the sky's surface:
faintly violet, touched with blue,
they lift the world to morning.
Time floods the senses.
Water is lulled to silver
like a painted soup bowl.

Hanging over the circular net,
a face tumbles back from the green.
Beneath there is movement -
in the darkness creatures lie,
bodies dark and sleek,
moving over and under.

Out in the middle, water changes tempo,
moves to a boiling,
frenetic, awash with life.
Teeming in the sudden sunlight,
their bodies given rounds and smooths,
salmon flash and fret, flicker and fly.

Scales caught in white light,
burnished backs,
bellies slimly silver,
these fish are dancing:
black shadows changed
to weaving arcs of light.

Swept by watered silk,
surrounded by wired net,
they are trapped and raised,
yet there is grace and freedom.
Their bodies tuned to a tale
of water; spirits pulsing.

Moths in Autumn

There are moths at the window,
aflutter like leaping flames,
knocking in a frenzy of wings
and legs and small soft heads.

Insistent as the soft tick
at the wrist - that shadowed
leap of skin, blue-hued
and tremulous as a first kiss.

Their legs beat a staccato tattoo,
their thrumming growing more
persistent as the night darkens;
a wild desire building.

For how long do moths live?
To grant only one day and night
to these furred and fragile creatures,
this vibrant pulse at the glass.

In the morning I hunt
for their small bodies,
seeking the stained path,
the faint mark of their fall.

There is only absence in the garden:
flowers and leaves stilled,
the breath of the wind held,
as if waiting for dusk -

for small, winged acrobats
to thicken the air, shudder
the light motes, stirring the silence
with their impassioned, tumbled flight.

Hoar Frost

In the cold mornings
there is frost at the windows
making stars and daggers
and hazy, pitted patterns.
Along the rail, pale spikes form,
catching the light like diamonds.
So this is hoar frost:
this turning of the world to jewels.
The snow stands up,
a fierce glistening;
the ground is transformed,
its tumultuous glittering
a valiant waving of spears
like crystalline thistles.

Books For Dreaming

Heavy and crisp,
they lie in my lap
like monuments.
They assault my heart,
turn my limbs to liquid:
my eyes collide with cliff, volcano,
I am caught in the limbs of trees,
stumble on tiny lichens,
drown in the dark eyes of bears,
I run after the black flap of raven in the woods,
watch the swift, ghost-step of grey wolves passing,
or else, the brown sweep of rivers drains on the page,
washing my body to dirt, to soil,
my hair floating like the span of a delta,
or luminous marble rises
in the shape of temple, statue, pavilion,
containing me, shaping me
in cold, fluid forms.
Streaming across page after page
and into my fingers
is the lure of these things.
Sometimes, there's the scent of a 4000 year old tree
shifting in the paper,
or the hard, fading bark under my palm,
or small sand grains riffling in the corners of the book,
scratching at my skin and eyes.

Here, in my own house on the side of this mountain,
where violets creep
and frogs call brokenly,
I turn the pages of these books
and my body deserts me,
changes from solid to liquid, becomes porous; ether.
I escape like clouds,
gathering, dispersing,
in an endless chase after the world.

III

Reflections on the desert while remembering Argos

Agamemnon's poppies burn red against
the marble whiteness of rocky hillsides:
bright gobbets of blood heralding death,
yet birth bubbling too, welling in pockets
of time, flowering again and again.

The rock is ancient here, earth smeared
red and orange, sun caught and folded
in the soil. That whiteness is absent - age
resounds in this southern light, a yellowing
of the centuries like worn out parchment.

Red soil harbouring the past, each
grain of sand riffling, breeze-blown
like the sails of a Greek ship;
stories compressed and bloodied,
trodden deep into the stony ground.

Poppies don't bloom here - their red
essence distilled years ago into the ochre
land, beads of blood staining the surface.
Other kings have been murdered here
these hillsides murmur with their sighs.

Ceramics / Braille

for Jane

Eyes closed, fingers braced to earth
and fire; the darkness carries tides
of light as skin and pores blossom:
trace veins, the pulse of the world.
Sand grains, water-rush, fire's heat:
taste this cauldron of years - drop
after drop of ancient water melding
soil, leaf, bark, stone, white clay.
And in cold stone, hear the voices,
thin whisperings taking flight,
stories tumbling against each other;
faint bird call echoing on the wind.
Hear the featherbrush, wingtip-touch,
the frail, unfurling frond and grass,
the fragile, porcelain-blue of shell
against dark strength of woven reed.
Deep in the soil the peat thickens,
the steaming earth's rich hoardings:
crush of damp ferns, crumbling moss,
burning embers, coal and hard twig.
Raised to exactness of fingerprints,
the whole world is lit transparent
until muteness speaks in many tongues;
the heart's pulled taut, listening to
the world spoken through these hands.

Kata Tjuta

Many heads ringed together:
a field of burgeoning mushrooms
stained red and golden in the spilling light.

Looming above, they are red scavengers;
birds with folded wings
blocking out the blue loophole of sky.

Shadowed clefts bud with water,
luminous green bursts like unfolding
umbrellas during a rain squall.

These heads are domed and soporific -
a dazed people emerging from the soil.

Mountains

These mountains are saturated with blue -
an echo of the ocean's depths,
water-filled and resonant,
ink-stained and silent.

Blue-black of metal and mosque tile,
coal and slate, duskiness of otter
pelt and mole skin, the pluming
whorl of crow feather and smoke.

They are etched and blooming with dye,
stained like a printer's fingertips,
stone-bright and veined as irises,
indigo horses high-stepping.

They well and rise, plum-blue,
soft as shadows or the matt-
velvet wings of bats
that float and swell at dusk.

Earth and sky fade in a hazy
wash, blending edges, blurring
outlines, until land tumbles
skyward endlessly - a mirage

of fields of cornflowers, orchards
of sloes, beds of sapphires,
roofs of lapis lazuli; a massing
torrent of ink, of ocean, of blue.

Night-Sky
for Rolan

You have been waiting a long time for this.
Every night we leave the white blinds open
and let the dark come pouring in.
Before sleep you scan the sky,
above the water and distant hills,
for light,
then as sleep settles,
your breath suggests your search.

Tonight the dark receded
and there, in watery, green brilliance
like the sea's reflection in a silver mirror,
were the lights you've longed for.
The vast bowl of the sky ignited from within:
a dance of fireflies,
swarming and darting
then arching with a flame-thrower's fire.

We stood in the crisp air,
the night a mantle on our shoulders,
and watched the heavens glow
with a shell-pink tinge,
and I heard the word dawn
deep inside of you:
      aurora.

Storm, Jervis Bay

The sky is clam-blue, mussel-dark,
massing and massing
to violet
to violence.
It hisses, seethes,
a lava-dark boiling,
richer than paint,
heavier than dam water
caught behind layered concrete.
This singing sky -
a thousand mad insects
humming, clicking;
the constant whir of wings.
Sound fractures,
the air thrums thickly
as clouds weight and sail,
piling fat as winter eiderdowns;
dark as the bruised heart of plums.

———————

As the sky collapses
the dam's unleashed:
lightning tearing like an arrow
aimed at the heel of the world.

This streak, this plunge,
this is the fissure
dividing the real and the illusory;
a blind hand peeling back the firmament
to the silent spinning of atoms.

Mycenae

Outside, bees dart or hover,
tiny feet whir against pollen.
They find pungent flowers,
lie against the petals like velvet dots.

I remember poppies,
fragile in the breeze,
bobbing like red-coated soldiers.
Against the whitened rock
they were flags of blood,
blooming, staining, startling.
Mesmerized, I wandered,
wanting to pluck and gather armfuls.

Our path wound around the hill
to the tombs of Mycenae,
which rose like yellow domes,
baked to a softness in the sun.
Above us, bees hovered,
they swarmed against the ceiling,
the walls, amber honeycomb.

The bees were black as poppy stamen,
velvety stems clustering
at the heart of the hive-like flowers,
drawing the eye inwards to the core

until tomb and flower were suns
bursting with yellow heat,
absorbing the self in this spiralling,
sundance of the eye.

Honey pools on my spoon,
rolls of redness, sticky as the sun;
for a moment, beehive tombs
and poppies crush in my mouth -
Mycenae rises rich and oozing,
a gold memory dissolving on my tongue.

IV

Hurt

I

In Florence it was the pigeons
flocks of them
strutting, pecking
seeking the warm crumbs from my palm.
If I stood still long enough
my body slowed to the fixity of marble -
a somnolent David
the anchored hooves of the Trevi Fountain -
and they would come to me
disciples, hungry children
wanting the small seed pearls.
In parks and squares
my body full of munificence
like a flowering field of corn
and always I'd cry for the one-legged bird
the lame, the picked-upon.

In Rome it was the cats.
One in particular
haunted my footsteps.
I would miaow and purr
scratch its bent, bitten ears
feed it when older faces turned away.
It came to love me I think

and I dreamed of cat-smuggling
across Europe, across borders.
On the final day
it came with presents
tossed a tiny bundle into the van.
My father swiftly kicked it out
and I fled, crying
for the tiny kitten-gift
the broken faith.

II

In the eyes of every animal
is a child
and an old man or woman.

I remember a ballet student
who held the perfect swan-flight
of an arabesque
jettéd with jaguar-abandon
pirouetted and floated
with animal grace.

Yet in the changeroom
her slender body slowly encased
in black leotard
her limbs
tawny and lithe
she described

night-shooting
aiming at the soft ears
of a possum
one
by
one
its brush tail
and finally
its heart.

She laughed.

And I cried inside
at the knowledge
of the brown
fragile eyes.

The Wedding Dress

Shrouded in a plastic bag,
breathing its own fading scent,
it lay at the top of my mother's cupboard.
Occasionally she would take it out,
pull the folds of ivory fabric from the bag.
It pooled like petals, waxy as flowers,
falling away in layers and ripples;
seas shifting under our fingers.
It was rose-blown,
fragrant with age and solemnity,
casting a spell like the forbidden camellias
in our father's garden.
The skirt belled, and dragged its regal train
in a heavy cascade of satin,
the neck scooped low on shoulders
and the bodice was nipped from breast to waist.
At twelve, the zip just zipped,
and there in the glass was an unreal figure,
fragile as a flower.

Later I would lift the dress with silent, secret fingers,
discard school uniform for its cool mantle,
wriggle and ease shoulders, breasts,
then inch the zip from waist to ribcage.
How my fifteen year old body cried
at the undone space where pale flesh showed.

I would breathe in and breathe out,
twist and stretch,
but all the flowers on the fabric
turned their accusing faces at me,
as if I had trodden the sacred ground of the camellias,
touched their petals
and turned their pearl-shell beauty to brown.

Delusions

Flaxen and floating I saw myself, soft
as gossamer, blown in intricate
circles like a dusky moth, aloft,
winged and free-wheeling in the air.
Toes, elfin and pointed, slender arms
encircling the sky, graceful as branches,
long, willowy and charmed -
catching the world in my hands.
Mimic of my sister: in pink kid shoes
and puff white tutu, she was a silken
creature I had to catch, I could not lose,
yet I was a twirling minstrel next to her.
In bright and ragged colours, just a clown;
the spiky thistle seedpod to her soft thistledown.

Awakening

World swamped by blueness of sea and sky,
your breath, wind-cooled, eddied at my mouth,
your eyes above me were bursts of indigo dye
like erupting spinnakers or birds flying south.
Skin-smooth, snail-soft, your lips left trails,
anemone-mouth insistent as a child's,
messages drowned on my body like sea tales;
gentling my flesh, you whispered and beguiled.
Sky floated above like an open umbrella,
we were lost there in that limbo of blue,
the wind breathed out the word *forever*
and at the heart of it there was only you.
We hovered, bodies anchored to warm stone,
spirits chasing sky and air; each alone.

The Dominic Poems

madonna, 1995
for Bronwen, seven months pregnant

Your belly balloons like a blown-glass bowl
- Murano glass bluely fracturing the light,
concave reflections of lagoon water
catching in the corners of the city,
sliding into rooms, paintings, portraits.

Body buoyant, belling and blue-veined
- Mary's blue skirts belled also,
white hands resting calm, smoothing
the nap of the velvet folds, her eyes
serene, dark hair filled with lagoon-light.

Your stomach is melon-round, and ripe
as the oranges we drank from
in the dark green hue of a Greek orchard,
your brown hair haloed in the half-light;
a Byzantine Madonna.

Body seeded in the sailing wind
- that faint breeze shifting our hair
as we climbed the endless steps
to Palamida, watching for Greek sails
to glide in at the harbour.

Your silhouette rides the swelling air
just as our boat rode the waves
of the Blue Grotto; sea light casting
its glow on wall and face alike,
blueness seeping into your eyes.

Body as sleek and polished as an olive,
burnished and blooming, ancient
as a Mediterranean Madonna
of fresco, mosaic or painting, but fleet
with the airy light of the present.

from womb to world
for Dominic Jackson Prazak, born 17th June 1995

New as a Christmas pea,
small, pale and smooth,
you slipped your pod,
rolling your roundness
into our lives.

Like a baby mole, blind
and silent, soft-pelted,
you burrow for a familiar
darkness, snuffle
for a lost sweetness -

the unsung song,
soundless, rolling hum
that whales sing.
In your private ocean
you floated and dived,

testing tiny limbs
in a watery world,
circling yourself, wary
of the far shore
and the shallows.

Oblivious to air
and land, you spun
and twirled; a small

sea urchin slowly
shedding your shell.

Your tight eyes and soft nose
strain for watery music -
the mermaid's melody
that was your lullaby,
your kenning.

Now you nestle deep,
sucking at the sweetness
that dives you back
merging land and sea,
air and brine,

turning you to turtle,
seal, sliding from
realm to realm
with milk and sleep
and milk again.

Slowly, your skin seeks
the dry air, your eyes
the light, until there is
only a faint, lilting wash
at the heart of things.

in the bath

There is my body -
legs thrusting to the porcelain rim,
knees riding the surface wash,
breasts bobbing beneath my chin,
bottom bumping the rounded floor,
arms darting like small minnows.
It is anchored in the shallows,
rocking and keeling in the soap-
water; homely as a house boat.

And there is your body -
small pink fists colliding,
toes pointing in all directions,
tummy arching and rising,
then swooping to the deep.
You are abandoned, light
as mushrooms and palely white;
small piece of flotsam, afloat,
like a tiny, wooden child's boat.

Your blue eyes stare,
reflecting water, air, sky,
we wriggle our toes, raising them
like the backs of hippopotami
in murky African rivers.
We sail smoothly on, our bath
a vast ocean, uncharted paths
through wild and absorbing lands -

so much water under our command.

Your small lips blow,
pursing like a fish's mouth,
hands smacking tiny waves
as you turn your body south,
heading for tropical islands,
my body bumping ungainly after.
Your face dissolves in silent laughter
as you bob and rise and toss,
light and airy as fairy floss.

Suddenly, you are lifted
clear away in your mother's hands,
she swoops you from water to towel -
the tropics only a dream of sands
sifting in the wind. There is
no longer your bobbing whiteness,
your companionable toes - only silence
and this boat becalmed and searching
in the shallow, cooling water.

Miracle

Here is the heartland,
this blown perfection
that mirrors earth, moon,
the horizon curving to roundness.

Slow as a ghost you turn,
fingers webbing the liquid air,
blind to the world like a salamander
but alive to wind-sift, sea-thrust.

Limbs like fishes,
pale and far away
as the man in the moon,
yet anchored deep;

your radiance spreading out,
turning woman to pulsing sun.

Fossils

for Patrick,
born 12th May 1998

In that cold stone
leaves furl their living skins
bending and stretching as if breeze-borne still.

Permian/Triassic
names that ring with the blood-lust of rock
alive with the haunting call of the long-dead.

They are embedded like jewels
their veins striated
like rainforest fronds from home.

As we stoop to gaze
your tiny fingers unfurl
waving in the winter air like leaves

sending a race of new blood
to stretch and thunder
in your limbs and eyes.

Fingers alive to the sky's endlessness
to the constancy of atoms
catching the breath of trees

escaping
for now
the hunger of stone.

Relics

for Lawrence,
born 16th August 2000

Poised above you,
I watch the tiny line of your jaw,
the fine down dancing
as milk slides in your throat.
You are small as a marsupial,
your jaw's outline polished like stone;
clear as white bone.

Outside, the ocean's slow churn,
its wash against the hollow rocks below,
is your suck and swallow at my breast.
The sea tosses up rounds of kelp,
ropes of weed and wrack to lie like wreaths
burnt by the cold air;
the colour of your dark hair.

Nestled in one mound
is the sickle of a jawbone.
Against brittle seaweed
it has the strength of centuries
- your mothlike tremor and pulse absent -
but it is bleached to the lightness of wind;
weightless as your breath on my skin.

Coracle:

part coral
part ache
part leak with a c
then there's lore and oracle too

and somewhere, beyond the letters on the page
is the deep hollow of a walnut
the dark shadowed heart of it
minus the flesh
womb-like
and the rock of it is womb-like too

it rides the water
a gentle bird-flight
waves lapping like velvet
their smoky wetness
like the first water
the green fluid
this could be the child tumbling
slow turning towards the light

it makes its quick passage
out of the harbour
night sky fleet with stars
it is sail-less, rudderless
just this tiny craft

bobbing and rising through the black water
the fathoms of liquid heavier than air

tiny as a child's palm
wooden hull ropey as a kernel
the gold colour lost in the blackness
like a flame snuffed out
but small bubbles spill in its wake
white and milky as pearls

it is a basket made for cargoes of preciousness
imagine rose petals
their soft colour lifting in the breeze
scenting the waves
or the small body of a child heavy with sleep
its limbs like the pale buds of flowers

where are the rushes and the lilies?
this is no river or pond
this is fast water running to the sea
out there are stars, whole galaxies
the spinning of the earth

this could be the first journey
or the last

Coastlines

Islands are coracles are memories
are sand and stone:
this eating of the heart,
soft flesh dissolving.
These shores
where driftwood lies like bones,
the flotsam shifts and settles:
seed pearls.
Note the pulpy centre of seaweed,
golden chambers of seawrack
like cathedral naves
with God's light pouring warm,
molten metal, blown glass.
Such softness and sunlight,
intricacies of rain,
the porous grains absorbing
shafts of water green as glass,
fluid as blood
that passes and enters,
floats and runs.
This body on the shore,
that boulder perched at eye level,
those cliffs alive with the restlessness of soil,
the shifting murmur of rocks.
The speech of the world
whispered and nudged on the wind:

grey petals of sky
come folding, fading,
forming concavities;
an archipelago of silence.

Stone Boat

Here is another coracle,
stone-walled, solid,
no flying reeds or endless sinking spaces.

It floats in a sea of black lines,
suspended, caught
like a fly in sticky honey.

The oars part the blackness,
dipping deep
or are they merely skating on the surface,

guiding it swiftly
like Orlando's Russian lover's boat
caught in Thames' ice.

How the towers rise,
straight-walled,
their windows

like small puckers of wind,
dark eyes,
the hearts of flowers.

A whole city casting off,
drifting purposefully away and out;

a barge, a galleon.

How many sea journeys
begin like this,
crossings, passages:

moving through dark water
to the silent, white spaces
at the edges of the mind.

Lines from the Black Sea

Banishment is a harsh word.
It scrapes its knuckles across the tender lining
of the ear - hard at first, then hissing insidiously,
like the wind pouring through the stunted branches of
    these trees.
It is a word beginning in blue, ending in black,
dark as these endless, winter nights.

Banishment jumps and halts on the tongue
in just the way this gutteral, Getic language
stumbles and falters forwards.

How I long for the polished glide of Latin,
smooth as skinned and pitted grapes
exploding in my mouth,
the sensuous rub of words,
silken as the sheen of oil over skin.

———————

I dream of cities,
their marble arches and stone streets
glowing in the summer heat.
I yearn for cool, crisp linen
washed to whiteness, dyed to deepening purple
and the suppleness of soft leather on my feet.
I desire the dark eyes,
the brazen mouths,
the gold bracelets on bare, brown arms
of Roman women.

———————

My body is failing me.
In this chill, foreign air
I grow dizzy with fatigue,
my eyes fumble in the thin light,
my knees feel the ache of cold.
My body is as fickle as Augustus himself.

———————

The fishermen here unfurl their nets
into the vast sea -
it stretches away from us,
a kind of infinite being,
omnipotent as an Emperor.
Its whims grant us silver fish for dinner -
grilled on hot coals they are delicious,
better than a banquet in their spareness.
There is a leanness here,
a paring back to bone,
to the pearly white essence of things.

———————

If I had a boat
and the strength to sail it
I could make my way home.

Return to the lithe, summer air,
to the cool breath of early evening,
to amber wine on my tongue.

I would navigate the narrow channels,
the inland waters, as if they were
the warm, secret places of my lover's body.

I would suffer the storms of open seas
as if they were the wild gasps,
the frenzy of our couplings.

I would breast the coast of my country,
hugging every inch and crook
as if breathing love into the pores of her body,
cajoling with my lips and tongue
until, at last, we arrive at Rome.

———————

The silver fish
echo and glisten
like the falling notes
of a young boy's voice.

———————

Sometimes
when winter crowds in
and my heart stops
its fierce clamouring for a second
I think of the long darkness
the endless Winter
the *ad infinitum* hibernation.

———————

When these people hunt and kill
where does the soul of the beast fly,
do its eyes tremble and fix on the horizon
as the knife plunges in,
does its mind trip and spin
in a crazy flight,
heading to where the sky moves to thin parings of silver
at the very edge of this black sea?

———————

In spring small shoots appear,
the soft, white heads of flowers,
and the tight, young green of grasses.

My body responds as if new blood
streams through its veins
a strong coursing like mountain snow-melt
running to the sea.

I don't remember spring in Rome:
it seemed an endless summer -
everything golden and melting,
pliant and malleable,

and coming to an end.

Notes to the poems

Jack Carington Smith: this eminent Tasmanian painter, a winner of the Archibald Portrait Prize and a lecturer in Art at the University of Tasmania, had a holiday cottage at Simpson's Bay on Bruny Island, where he undertook much of his painting.

The Garden: the word 'paradesh' is Persian for paradise, meaning a walled garden surrounding a palace. Vita Sackville-West established her garden at Sissinghurst, part of which is the famous White Garden. She was close friends with Violet Trefusis and Virginia Woolf.

Meditative Sonnets: these grew out of a conversation with the painter Kerry Gregan, with whom I was paired for the Poets and Painters Exhibition in memory of Gwen Harwood, which was part of the 1996 Salamanca Writers' Festival.

Ceramics/Braille: this poem was written for the ceramist, Jane Bamford, who had it translated into braille by members of the Hobart Braille Library. Jane then printed it onto large square ceramic platters, a technique she developed herself.

Relics: Genevieve Cox's photograph, 'Beached,' was the impetus for this poem. The poem and photograph were exhibited at The Republic, Hobart, as part of the 2000 Women Poets and Artists Collaboration, organised by Liz Winfield.

Coracles and *Coastlines:* conversations on sculptor Ward

Knight's boat were the starting point for these two poems. Ward and I collaborated for the 1997 Poets and Painters Exhibition at the Dick Bett Gallery, Hobart.

Stone Boat: this is a response to a print of the same name, by Neil Moore, and grew out of the work with Ward Knight.

Lines from the Black Sea: the Roman poet Ovid, who was exiled to the Black Sea by Emperor Augustus, is the speaker.